The Art of Staying Out the Way
The Book

by Andre Smith

edited by BreAuna Jackson

t.a.o.s.o.t.w

a DreSmitti creation

Published by Andre Isley Smith Publications

Copyright © 2015 by Andre I. Smith

All rights reserved. This book or any portion thereof may not be reproduced or used in any manner whatsoever without the express written permission of the publisher except for the use of brief quotations in a book review.

Andre Isley Smith Publications

Chicago, IL 60651

andreismithpub@gmail.com

Library of Congress Control Number: 2015950713

ISBN-13: 978-0-9967472-0-2

Cover design by Pixel Dizajn

Cover photo by Andre I. Smith

Images by Andre I. Smith

Printed in the United States of America

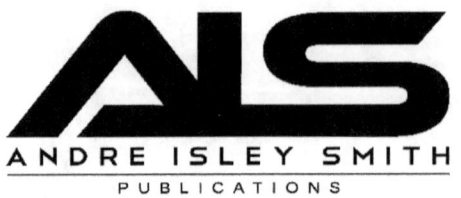

Contents

Dedication i

Mission Statement ii

Preface iii

Acknowledgements v

Introduction 1

   I.   **That Dark Place** 4
        Westside of Chicago   5
        Physical features   6
        Mental features   15

   II.   **Maneuver #1: Boss Up** 21
        Think like a boss   22
        Since 3rd grade   24
        From the 'hood to college   25

   III.   **Maneuver #2: Move Differently** 30
        Move like a boss   31
        Fast money addiction   33
        Crackin' Cards   35

   IV.   **Maneuver #3: Good Vibes Only** 41
        Haters, doubters, bad company, etc   42

        Hating on the job   45

        Good vibes   52

V.   **Maneuver #4: S O L O** 54

        Faith   55

        Home, navy or college   56

        The Westside Fraternity   59

VI. **Maneuver #5: Remind Yourself** 64

        Identify, learn and grow   65

        Pause!   65

        Introduced to gangs   67

        A "FeFe" out west   70

VII. **Maneuver #6:** Stay out the way & Work! ... 77

        Stay out the way   77

        Stay working   79

Last Encouraging Words 82

Pledge on Staying Out the Way 83

The Worksheet 85

Summary 91

Dedication

This book is dedicated to the memory of the young boys and girls whose lives were shortened by gun violence. I am sure that they all had something great to offer the world, but unfortunately they were not alive long enough to reveal their gifts. In their memory I am dedicated to giving as much as I can to the world as long as I am breathing.

Mission Statement

As a young black male who has come from a dark place and who is constantly provoked by the darkness, both physically and mentally, it is my mission to help give light to those who are caught in the darkness. I will openly share whatever services and wisdom that I have with those who seek it. As a young black male, I will continue to learn more about myself. I will always remain true to who I am and what I believe. I will remain honest with God, myself and with those who love me. Patience is crucial, so I will maintain faith throughout my process of becoming a complete man. As a young black male, I will define me, not the media or society. Success is inevitable. When it is all over, I envision that I have made my God and my family proud of me. My plan is to leave something behind that could be shared amongst people from all walks of life.

Preface

Throughout my life, I have attained a great deal of achievements through my own trial-and-error. In the beginning, I never know exactly how to do things or how I should appear as I'm doing it. I become stagnant and hesitant as a result! I either hesitate to follow-through with a great idea or remain trapped in my undeveloped ways. Until one day, I decided to stop asking God for riches. On this day and every day going forward, I've decided to ask God for a clearer vision and more wisdom instead. I was 25 years old when I made this change.

It took me 25 years to understand that with a clearer vision and more wisdom I could improve the person I am, do whatever I want and possibly become wealthy. God can't bless me with things that he didn't create himself. Money and material things are man-made. God only gives us the opportunities to obtain those things if they're meant for us to have. Instead, God has blessed me with two tools that could fix any situation and these tools are vision and wisdom. With these universal tools I have faith that I could fix any flaw.

Keep in mind that I didn't honestly make this transition until I was 25 years old. I'm surprised at how long I survived without asking God for these two important tools. As a young black man who was raised in the 'hood, how was I able to avoid death and prison while being partially lost? The answer is that God had mercy on me, so he blessed with a great awareness level and survival instincts at a very young age. With the addition of my improved wisdom and vision, I've been able to reflect and understand exactly how I had recognized and practiced *The Art of Staying Out the Way* throughout my life.

Acknowledgments

Above all, I want to acknowledge God because it is God who makes all things possible. In all my ways, I acknowledge God. God knows best and has made all my paths straight. My faith and trust for God goes beyond measure. God has blessed me abundantly and I am truly thankful for each blessing. I am most thankful for the amazing mother that God has blessed me with. Without my mother, my journey would've been so much harder. Without God's mercy, my life would've been so much shorter. God I know it is you who supply all my needs. I can do all things through Him who strengthens me. Please continue to have mercy on me as I strive to become the person that you know that I could be.

Special Thanks.

Special thanks to my parents (Andre M. Smith and Alexis Y. Davis), my grandparents (Robert Smith, Frank Davis, Barbara Davis and Louise Smith), my sister (Adrienne Hayes), my entire family, Coach Space, Mr. McKay, Tshaura, the Cobb family, the Savage family and close friends for inspiring and supporting me. Last but not least, thank you BreAuna Jackson for your editorial assistance.

Introduction

The Art of Staying Out the Way is offering maneuvers that will enable you to *stay out the way* of society's barriers, pitfalls, traps and evils. Specifically, I'm referring to you avoiding any negative and damaging situations that either leaves you miserable, penniless, lifeless or incarcerated. This book will introduce exactly what the phrase *staying out the way* entails. *Staying out the way* is an *art* in every sense because it requires creative and technical skill. My goal is to share my vision and wisdom with you about this skill, so that you could use it as a life tool for yourself.

The Art of Staying Out the Way will provide a description of what makes a dark place such a challenging place for anyone to reach their full potential while surrounded by the darkness Also, many other situations share similar barriers, pitfalls, traps and evils. With this in mind, everything shared in this book should be translatable for a variety of readers. I will share some of my best practices for maneuvering through such situations. I am firm believer in the fact that if you're able to make it out of a dark place, then you are more than capable of making it anywhere else.

The Art of Staying Out the Way should apply to whomever despite character distinctions. Also, this book applies to whomever regardless of the uniqueness of their dark place. A dark place is either an internal condition such as your self-esteem, mentality and spirituality. Or it could an external condition, such as career situation, living condition and school situation. Essentially, a dark place is considered dark whenever there's either evilness, unfortunate difficulty or a high level of uncertainty present. We must first learn The *Art of Staying Out the Way* of any harmful situations, disadvantageous pitfalls, unhelpful traps, unnecessary trouble and other evils in order to become successful.

While reading this book, it's important for you be open and reflective. Our ways of thinking are shaped by our personal experiences and observations. Also, the way we receive information is shaped by the same. I must admit that this book is partially shaped by my lived experiences and observations. Therefore, my thoughts are shared from a personal and professional perspective, but I remained as honest and reflective as plausible. There are maneuvers that I've learned and practiced over the course of my journey. They have helped me *stay out way*. However, the maneuvers offered in this book are transferrable to anyone's situation.

Each following chapter will offer maneuvers that you could use for gradually bettering your position in life and they are meant to sharpen the moves that you're already making as well.

It is very important that you hone *The Art of Staying Out The Way* considering the many barriers, pitfalls, traps and evils that all exists out there in society. Once again, every maneuver offered in this book is transferrable. And hopefully my testimonies are relatable to others' personal and/or professional experiences.

The Art of Staying Out the Way

Westside of Chicago, IL 2015

That Dark Place

We have all experienced a dark place at some point in life. This dark place could have been either physically, mentally, or spiritually disturbing. Specifically, a dark place is filled with uncertainty, pain, evilness, unhappiness, danger, failure, anger, desperation, losses, and other negative features. Physically, a dark place could be a broken home, jail, an unfulfilling job and/or an unsafe neighborhood. Mentally, a dark place could be a person's blurred thoughts about committing suicide, homicide or other criminal acts. Metaphorically speaking, a person could feel as if there's a dark cloud floating over him/her. Internally, this person may feel hopeless, depressed, and unlucky. The darkness may overwhelm a person and, as a result, he/she may begin to believe that God doesn't favor him/her. Whenever people completely lose faith in themselves and God, then this is the darkest place for any person to exist. But once again, we've all been in a dark place before. Some of us made it out, but others still remain in the darkness. If you're anything like me, then you've made it out of the darkness and before long were threatened by it again and again. The darkness has plenty barriers, pitfalls, traps and evils. I've experienced the darkness both physically, mentally and spiritually. However, there was one particular dark place that I've experienced where I'd honed several maneuvers while evading its barriers, pitfalls, traps and evils.

Certain areas of Chicago's Westside have had a dark cloud floating over it since the late 1960s. While residing in this dark place, I was totally surrounded by darkness. Fortunately, I had God, family and friends while in this dark place. Together, they all provided some light for me as needed. They acted as my night lights as I made my way through the darkness. However, in order for you to better understand the setting where I honed majority of the maneuvers that I'm offering in this book, I will share some observations of the physical and mental features that are visible on Chicago's Westside.

The Physical Features

It does not get any darker than the urban neighborhoods of Chicago, such as the Holy City. The Holy City is a Chicago neighborhood that was historically made into a headquarter for a dominant gang that was founded by several African American youths in the 1960s. Liquor stores, drug addicts, gangs, guns, fast food restaurants, corner stores, broken glass, broken schools, broken homes and vacant lots are a few descriptions for this dark place. In a vacant lot you may either see a group of elderly guys still holding onto habits that they've had since they were younger, or you may witness a group of kids playing baseball, football and tag on top of scattered-broken glass. Also, in this vacant there are either some abandoned cars that were stripped, or cars that were parked there in order to avoid getting booted by the city. During night hours this dark place becomes much darker and, in a vacant, you may see huge rats hunting for food that never reached a garbage container.

If you were to take your eyes away from this vacant lot and scan them to your left or right, then there is a great chance you may see gangs embracing street corners like basemen embrace bases in baseball. These gang members are usually in flashy uniforms that represent their team is winning, such as flashy jeans with designs stitched onto the back pockets, designer belts, fashionable gym shoes, etc. The names of their home field are inspired by the names of old members who were retired by death. The size of their home field covers like a two-three block radius at the most. But what's a game without referees? The police watch these corners like base umpires in baseball. Their job is to determine whether these corners are "safe" or if there are players "out" hustling and causing trouble at these particular corners.

Gang members ball together and inevitably fall together due to the police locking them out the game or rivals sending bullets their way quicker than fastballs. Instead of nine innings, these players play the field indefinitely, but have short careers. For this reason, the recruitment season is all-year long in order for the gangs to remain strong.

Prospective gang members are normally children recruited out of broken homes and/or broken schools. These broken homes are generally fatherless and poverty-stricken. Government welfare is expected to help fix the homes of these poverty-stricken families. Instead, welfare deliberately handicaps these families who have grown dependent on government assistance. This dependency causes families to methodically abuse the welfare program because they choose to remain unemployed, have more children, or stay unmarried in order to qualify for greater benefits. Despite families being on welfare, they are still poverty-stricken and their living conditions are inhumane indefinitely.

There are specific tasks that families must gradually achieve throughout its family's cycle in order to develop their children into happy, successful members of the family. The development of each family member influences other family members and, in the end, influences the overall growth of the entire family as well. In general, when a newborn is born, the task of the family is to provide a safe environment for the toddler to explore at this stage. Next, as this newborn grows into a young child, the family must achieve the task of continuing to provide a safe foundation for this child, but a more economical foundation rather than physical at this stage. Fundamentally, families are obligated to change and accommodate the needs of their children as they age.

Unfortunately, welfare hinders many families living in this dark place and these tasks are never or barely met. Instead of the mother accommodating her child's needs as he ages, she is idle while she awaits her next government check and Link Card balance to pop on monthly. The soon-to-be gang member will most likely be a child that is being raised in one of these broken/fatherless homes. Since birth, his environment has been unsafe and he's been poor, hungry and lost. Once noticeable, the hunger displayed by this affected child is favorable to gang scouts because the child's hunger for the finer things in life could be easily exploited by gang leaders.

These prospective gang members are more intrigued by what they could gain and learn in the streets and are less concerned with what is offered in their broken-public schools. So what makes these schools broken? Irrelevant curriculums, lowered expectations, violence, unconcerned teachers, overcrowded classrooms, lack of male teachers, scarce funding, etc. Inside these broken schools, they are generally labeled trouble-makers or failures by the 3rd grade and this label follows them to every subsequent grade. Specifically, these students are labeled as aggressive, violent, poor readers, or as classroom clowns. They are also known for lacking discipline and lacking respect for authority figures. These broken schools are not equipped with handy playbooks that could show these prospective gang members how to survive and score in the streets.

On a daily basis, these poor and uneducated children travel pass gang members who are "getting money". They notice that these gang members embrace each other's qualities, which are the same qualities that they are currently being criticized for possessing by their teachers. These social forces within the streets are unavoidable. As a result, these aspiring gang members view becoming gang member as an opportunity to join a team that fits them, and makes them feel important and valuable. After closely watching these gangs, shortly these aspiring gang members begin to hang out in front of stores that are also located near the corners where gangs generally do business. Generally, local residents shop at these corner stores for cakes, juice, candy, chips with cheese and meat, swishers, loose cigarettes and anything else unhealthy. While hanging in front of these corner stores, they start to ask questions, express interest and build relationships with active gang members. They are ready to play the game. As a result, from school they routinely begin to hang around on corners instead of going straight to their broken homes. Training camp is now in session.

During training camp, these aspiring gang members start selling drugs with their gang. This is the gang's primary source of business. Typically, their first position is "Security" or also known as "S". At this position, they alert everyone whenever the police are near the corner by yelling "LIGHTS". They soon become pack workers and start actively selling drugs themselves. Also, they began experimenting with drugs such as marijuana, alcohol, "lean" - a mix of prescription cough syrup with soda and candy – and ecstasy pills. While serving drug addicts, they also become one. By the earliest ages of 13-15, these aspiring gang members have graduated out of training camp and have become full-time drug-dealers and gang members. However, violence naturally comes along with being in a gang and selling drugs. They have to now carry guns or have one nearby while hustling because gunplay comes with the drug game.

Criminal behaviors are persistently reinforced in gangs. Daily, younger people in these gangs are being taught how to sell drugs, how to hide drugs, how to look out for the police, how to spot an opp' (opponent) and how to tuck their guns. Also, they are being trained to have attitudes of putting money before women, disliking the police, hustling hard, being ready to kill and so on. Ultimately, control and money is the motive and displaying unshakable loyalty for the gang is mandatory for every member in order for their team to dominate and win. A person becomes completely antisocial and overwhelmed by the darkness because their gang constantly advocates in favor of violating the law. This antisocial and gang lifestyle becomes all this person knows.

There are five roles that are commonly learned amongst children growing up in the 'hood. These following roles allow them to perform in this dark place:

1. **"Cool"** – Being cool is a lifestyle in the 'hood. Someone who is cool is normally up-to-date with clothing, lingo and is always familiar with recent events that have taken place in the 'hood. He knows everyone in the neighborhood, including gang members. Also, he finesses very well and, therefore, has an uncanny ability stay out of serious trouble. He has the ability to function under considerable pressure. He appears indifferent towards the problems that surround him by appearing to be insensitive to pain, frustration or death. The key to role is to remain relevant and cool beyond measures.
2. **"Send Off"** or **"A Goofy"** – Instead of being able to finesse his way out of serious trouble like someone that's cool, he learns to engage in the trouble. His role in the trouble is to behave foolishly in order to not appear weak and to be accepted. He's the clown and, ultimately, the "send off" in the 'hood. Seeing that he's a follower and willing to participate in any ill-behaved acts, he is used by the others guys as a scapegoat to do their dirty work. As a result, this person has plenty of run-ins with the law.

3. **"A Lame" or "A Cool Lame"** – He's the outcast in the 'hood. He resists gangs, drugs and other street norms. He's labeled a "good boy" or "a lame" by his peers. However, there are some "cool lames". The "cool lames" has successfully disassociated himself from gang activities yet still has maintained a distant relationship and respect with his peers. Ultimately, "the lame" must learn to live amongst gangs since they share the same dark place and social norms that directly has an effect on them all.

4. **"Cool, but not really out there like that"** – For the most part, he's accepted in the 'hood. He gets along with gang members, non-gang members and everyone else in the community. He is considered to be "one of the guys", but with limitations. He is typically good at a sport, such as basketball and/or football, which earns him some street cred'. He has middle-class dreams, but accepts his current living situation and deals with it accordingly. Therefore, he's non-judgmental of his peers and interacts with them very well. Essentially, he engages in activities in the 'hood, but never the activities that's too unsafe.

5. **"Savage"** – In particular, this is the guy that's on the most bullshit! Excuse my language, but he really eats, shits and sleeps bullshit endlessly. This dark place is definitely his playing ground and he takes full advantage

of it. As you might've noticed, my tone changed while writing about this guy and it's not because I strongly dislike him nor do I judge him as a bad guy. I tend to stay away from judging individuals as good or bad people. Instead, I judge them as having an obvious good spirit or evil spirit based on their actions. The savage is an individual with an evil spirit. He earns his street cred' from being able to outfight, intimidate or harass his peers. Eventually, he becomes a gang leader because of his heavy influence over others due to his ability to overpower people.

Gangs typically seek after savages and send offs, but a nice amount of the cool guys in the neighborhood may eventually join a gang as well because of the constant temptation. Still, others who are "cool, but not really on that" and cool lames often fall victim in this dark place as well. They reside amongst drugs and violence regardless of how uninvolved they are. When these gangs send gunshots quicker than fastballs in their rival gangs' direction, their aim is terrible and innocent bystanders get hit. Also, drugs are somehow introduced to almost everyone in this dark place. Some people try their first drug and, regardless of their previous innocence, they develop an addiction that directs them through a life of crime. Young guys with drug addictions gain their status in the 'hood by being the ones who frequently consume the most marijuana, Lean, and alcohol compared to their peers. In the 'hood, anyone could fall victim to drugs and violence.

The Mental Features

There are common ways of thinking amongst the people who reside in this dark place. In order to fully understand the hood's physical condition, then you must also be well-informed about the various mental states of the people who reside there:

1. **Hustlers' mindset** – At the expense of his freedom, he is willing to get money by all means while preying in this dark place. He is motivated by instant gratification. Education is placed on the backburner because it doesn't yield profit right away. In the year of 2015, the most common hustles practiced amongst hustlers are selling drugs and/or "cracking cards" – a bank fraud phenomenon. He is either willing to sell drugs to someone's mother or is prepared to take advantage of her daughter's bank account. Essentially, he has reduced the value of his life to a dollar. The hustler will choose death or jail before he'll ever settle with being broke. If it's not profitable, then it's not logical.
2. **The "it is what it is" mindset** – A person with this mindset arguably doesn't care much. He's tolerable with the gang and drug-infested conditions in this dark place.

His opinion about his environment and other similar environments are "black people gone continue to kill black people", "drugs gone be around forever, and there's nothing we could do about it", "I'm gone be in the hood forever", "I'm gone be the same person forever" and "that's just the way it is". In other words, his sense of hopelessness is masked as him being unmoved by or detached from his cruel living conditions.

3. **The "I'm the MAN in my 'hood" mindset** – This person aims to be a 'hood legend. He wants to dress the best, have sex with best looking females, drive the best looking cars and wants to be known by the most. In 2015, his car of choice is a foreign, an old school or van with 24-26 inch rims. He has to own a designer belt, buy new gym shoes every time they drop, wear flashy clothes and possess a gold chain with a Jesus piece. His is motivated to shine the brightest in this dark place.

4. **The "I'm gone do whatever to get it" mindset** – Similar to the hustler mindset, this person is just as willing to get money by any means. However, in his specific case, he is ready to get money by all means. He will commit armed robberies, home burglaries, auto thefts, sell drugs and other petty crimes for the love of the money. A person with this mindset just can't be

trusted, not even by his friends. According to him, "anybody could get it!"

5. **The "I hate working" mindset** – This person hates working menial jobs that pays minimum wages such as fast food restaurants, retail stores and supercenters. According to this person, "you can't make no real money" or "they try to work you like a slave" while working those types of jobs. Arguably, many of the jobs available to people living in the 'hood are actually exploitative. Conscious people with this mindset have legitimate arguments only if their disdain is motivated by this idea. However, a person with this mindset either will sadly find it more convenient to depend on government welfare assistance or to get money in the streets instead of working menial jobs for minimum wages.

6. **The "I hate school" mindset** – This person views school as boring and views what the teachers are teaching as irrelevant. According to this person, "school days are too long", the teachers don't like him, he believes he is not smart enough, making money is more important than him being at school and school is basically lame. Eventually, people with this mindset statistically add to this dark place's high school drop-out crisis and its uneducated population.

7. **The "I'm living in Hell" mindset** – This person is extremely hopeless. He chooses not to put his faith into anyone, anything or any religion. According to him, Hell is what he sees while living in this dark place and that's his reality. He lives life everyday welcoming any trouble that might come his way because he expects it. Ultimately, he views killing someone as a necessary option if he ever has to kill. It's not reasonable for him to try to live right in a place that's not right itself. This person doesn't believe in much and doesn't mind dying or killing. That makes this person most dangerous in this dark place.

8. **The "I rather be caught with it than without it" mindset** – This person prefer to get arrested by the police for having a gun instead of being caught without a gun by an enemy who has a gun and he gets shot as a result. In this dark place, the number of guns on the street is overflowing. There's so much gun violence and it appears as if everyone has a gun. This means that this person will keep a gun on him regardless of the almost definite consequence of him getting arrested for being in possession of one. If he's not on defense at all times, then he's in danger of not being able to shoot back whenever his enemies choose to come shoot at him while he's out on the block. According to this person, he

believes that his life desperately depends on him having a gun on person at all times.

9. **The "Ball until I fall" mindset** – This guy understands that death is inevitable, perhaps soon in his case. At one point, the expected expiration date for black males was the age of 21 in Chicago. In 2015, that age has fell to 19. This person wants to have non-stop fun, have sex with multiple females and splurge money on clothes, cars, drugs, designer clothes and gym shoes before his expiration date. He does not expect to live long because he knows of many friends and family members who have died at a young age. Also, his guilt eats away at his soul whenever he thinks of all the dirt he has done. He believes in karma and he is convinced that death or jail is around the corner. With this in mind, he's going to ball until his fall!

10. **The "Nobody cares about me" mindset** – This person has a total disregard for other people because he is convinced that people have a total disregard for his wellbeing. Nobody really cares about him; they just pretend to care. In his mind, his parents, family, teachers, probation officer and judge don't truly care about him. So he doesn't care who he disappoints nor does he care about those people that his actions affect. He feels alone. The hatred he has in his heart for people is vicious. He feels like people have failed him and, as a

result, they have left him in this dark place to defend for himself. Arguably, he might have a legitimate defense. Gangs typically take advantage of a person with this mindset. In many cases, this person life has a tragic ending.

The outcomes of a combination of these mindsets existing together in one dark place are the visible physical features. These features are violence, drug activity, auto thefts, home burglaries, littering, self hate, gang activity, guns, evilness, trouble and uncertainty throughout its environment. The problem is always much deeper than what it appears to be on the surface. It's crucial to search underneath the surface of a person in order to really understand their character and actions. Beyond the people, I am completely aware that oppression exists! There is no denying that. However, whenever there is combination of people living amongst each other with these types of mindsets, then the oppressors no longer have to actively inflict much harm against the oppressed as they did in the past. In the year 2015, we've reached a point where we're now doing majority of the damage to ourselves and there isn't anyone rushing to genuinely help us repair these damages. Therefore, we must learn to help ourselves. Once we begin to help ourselves, we then begin to help us.

The Art of Staying Out the Way

$$\begin{bmatrix} \text{Boss} \\ \text{Up} \end{bmatrix}$$

Maneuver #1

You have to boss up; point, blank, period! Allow me to expand on the meaning of "boss up". When I say "boss up", right away you might think that I'm referring to how you walk, dress, talk, look and what you do. Instead, I'm referring to your way of thinking. Learn to think like a boss. The level on which we think influences the level on which we strive to live. Currently, do you think like a boss? Are you the person in charge of your life or are you society's puppet? In order to walk, dress, talk, look and move like a boss, then you must first think like one. It's important that we become more aware and honest about our flawed ways of thinking. Until we realize and, then, change our flawed ways of thinking, we are going to continue to fall into the same traps and pitfalls. As a result, we will remain on the same level in life. The way we think controls they way we move.

So what's a "boss"? A boss is a person in charge. He/She controls what he believes in and what he stands for. He/She has goals and expectations set for himself/herself. Also, a boss knows or has an idea of what's beneficial and harmful for him/her. A boss's demeanor is shaped by a high level of self-worth. Along with confidence, a boss has great awareness. He/She does a great job of examining a situation thoroughly, so that he won't mistakenly place himself in a losing position. A boss has a mind of his/her own. God, family, progress and money all occupy a boss's mental framework, which leaves no space for unconstructiveness. Most importantly a boss values his/her mental wealth as well as financial wealth. Constant thinking is what allows a boss to constantly move up levels in life. However, a boss thinking is more rational than irrational. Every potential move is thought about realistically, so he/she considers favored outcomes as well unpleasing outcomes before making a decision.

What do I mean by "up"? In brief, the word "up" means to go from a lower to a higher point on something, or go to a higher price, value, or rank. It means to move into a desired condition as well as progress into a happy mood. Also, the word "up" means to move toward a higher position or to a place perceived as higher and to cause a level or amount to be increased. If your thinking isn't causing you to move up in life, then your thinking is flawed. In other words, if you wake up every day, week, month and/or year either dealing with the same negativity, drama or unfortunate situations, then you're obviously not moving in an upward direction. Remember, the only way to the top is up. Only true bosses understand that, in order to move forward in life, they must continue to boss up!

This might sound crazy or kind of corny, but I learned that life was all about bossing up at an early age. In Chicago's public schools, students could fail the 3rd grade. Well, at least that was the case back when I was in 3rd grade. As a 3rd grader at an elementary school located on the Westside, I enjoyed school mainly because I was there with my friends. The school work was annoying and boring at most times. However, when I made it to the 3rd grade, it made completely no sense for me to not do my class work and homework simply because it either boring or annoying. I did what I had to do to move forward! I refused to be in the same grade doing the same work the following year. Even though I had poor conduct grades each quarter that year in 3rd grade and almost every following grade, I made sure that I still completed more than enough class work and homework so that I could pass onto the next grade. As a result, I would not have to deal with that same grade, same class work, same homework, and/or same teacher the following year. This naturally made sense to me.

Fast forward, this type of thinking stuck with me as I went further in life as I applied it to more serious decisions that I had to make outside of school. My boss up mentality enabled me to be a forward thinker and, in the long run, allowed me not to become society's puppet. There was a situation in college. Pause, you probably thinking "here's another corny example", but this one is nothing like my 3rd grade example. Still, my 3rd grade discovery is the foundation for this following example. Anyhow this following example has nothing to do with school work, homework, or anything actually school related. I'll share some background information that's relevant for this next example. I went to college in a small town that was 60 miles away from the city during the years 2008-2013. I like to describe this place as "the city away from the city" because it seemed as if majority of the people from the Chicago area had chosen to drive 60 miles to this town to either attend college, party or reside during the period I was attending this college. Literally, it was like the 'hood moved to this small town. Guns, drugs, gangs, shootings, robberies, fights, fraud and so many other negative occurrences that are only expected to take place in the 'hood were in fact present in this so-called college town. The local police relentlessly enforced the law, so all criminal activity was short-lived. Despite the police successful efforts, people still tried to break the law. The buzz surrounding this specific college was broadly discussed. If a person lived in Chicago or went to another university in the state of Illinois, then there's a good chance they heard stories about the drama and parties that took place at this college during the years 2008-2013.

My sophomore year in college, there was some drama created amongst the group of guys that I'd normally I hung out with. In general, college is a clique-ish environment in nature and, therefore, my clique consisted of people who were all from the Westside of Chicago. You could describe us as the Westside fraternity. Basically, if a person was either from the Westside or was more connected with the Westside's culture, then they became a member of this fraternity. The drama amongst this fraternity was stirred up by a confrontational post on a social media website. This dude named Bleep, who was also a member of the Westside fraternity, made a post saying that certain members out of the fraternity was now banned from hanging out at his apartment for whatever reason that I can't recall. Bleep's apartment was in a location called "The Vill" and this was our official hang-out spot at the time when this post was made. All the card parties, pregame activities and after parties took place at Bleep's crib. Those now banned members took that post very seriously. A very controversial divide of the Westside Fraternity followed. It was those who were not banned versus those who were banned. I was one of the members who were not banned.

Petty posts on social media from both sides dissing each other and several fights ensued. There was one shooting and stabbing as the situation grew more controversial. Without exaggeration, there was a crazy brawl whenever we encountered each other. These fights took place in "The Vill", on college campus and at off-campus parties. Everyday someone either fought or something disrespectful was said on a social media website. I use to frequently express to both sides that they were "tweakin'". "Tweakin'" means that they were thinking irrationally and making bad decisions. However, I was immediately put in many situations that I had to defend myself even though I disagreed with what was going on because these fights occurred spontaneously. Eventually, I became fed up once

I further realized how messy and senseless we were. No matter how many times I tried to convince my guys that they were tweakin', they never listened. It was time for me to boss up! It was time for me to think rationally and realistically about my involvement and what was going on.

As I began to think more rationally about what was going on, I begun to think that none of it was worth it. Inside I'd always felt that way, but now I was completely fed up. In order to correct my actions, I had to think differently. Right away, I realized that many of those situations in which I initially thought I was unwillingly being forced to defend myself were an irrational thought. My flawed thinking ultimately led me into those situations. While fighting with my friends, I recognized that I was their puppet. I was put in situations I had no control over. I was fighting for something I did not personally believe in. For every fight that we won there was no monetary or personal gains. Also, our behavior was scaring away all the nice and pretty girls that I was personally attracted to. Our drama resulted in many loses and kept me on a lower level in life.

While reflecting, I had to remind myself that a boss controls what he believes in and what he stands for. A boss knows what's good for him and what's against him. Also, a boss does a great job of examining a situation thoroughly, so that he won't mistakenly put himself in a losing situation. Last, every potential move is thought about realistically, so this means I had to consider favored outcomes as well bad outcomes before making any decision going forward. Therefore, I chose to distance myself from my guys during this chaotic time. I started to spend more time with my girlfriend in order to avoid some of the confrontations that my friends were engaging in. Literally, my friends were waking up everyday looking for drama. That was not cool to me neither did it make any money nor sense. I begun to tell my guys I either had too much homework, or told them my girlfriend was cooking and taking care of me whenever they asked me to come out. Rationally thinking, my decision to distance myself from the drama was motivated by the thought that there wasn't anything for me to gain monetarily or mentally if I continued to contribute to the madness. If it does not help me go forward in life, then it is holding me back. That situation was holding me back, so I had to let it go.

From 3rd grade to my sophomore year in college and currently, I've always found it more beneficial to boss up. Bossing up is requires a person to think of better ways for moving forward in life. Prior to my college experience that I just shared with you, I experienced worse situations while growing up the 'hood. Life puts us in so many challenging situations that require us to constantly think our way out of or around these difficult circumstances. Bossing up has kept me alive and out of prison, which were my two most provoking traps and pitfalls. As I grow older, every subsequent challenge that I encounter requires me to think on a higher level in order for me to maneuver around various traps and pitfalls. Most importantly, as my mindset improves so does my life.

Use your better judgment and boss up. In order to maneuver your way out of troubling situations and into better ones, you must first improve your way of thinking. If you choose to think only about drugs, guns, violence and drama every day, then you will most likely surround yourself around drugs, guns, violence and drama daily. If you faithfully think about ways to be "the man" in the 'hood, then you will learn to do whatever it takes to be "the man" in your 'hood. Likewise, if you wake up daily thinking of ways to *stay out the way* and become successful, then you eventually learn plenty of ways for doing both. All I'm saying is this: whatever we put our mind to we could do it! I suggest you boss up!

$$\begin{bmatrix} \text{Move} \\ \text{Differently} \end{bmatrix}$$

Maneuver #2

Have you reached a point in life where you have grown tired of dealing with the same drama, same discontent and overall the same old lifestyle? Are you tired of making the same moves that lead you down a path to nowhere? If you wake up every day with your same unhelpful mentality, you will continue to deal with those same effects. That is why it is so important that you first "boss up"! Until we correct our flawed ways of thinking, we will continue to place ourselves in losing situations. Once again, we must become honest and self-reflective about why we are not where we want to be in life. I guarantee you will find that there actually are flaws in your current way of thinking and that these flaws are holding you back. The level we think on ultimately determines the level we strive to live on. In other words, our perceptions control our actions. Therefore, before you could even move differently, you must first think differently.

So you finally "bossed up"? From me to you, job well done! Now you are on your way up. Your growth will be inevitable. There is no way for you to *stay out the way* without first changing how you think. Instead of walking into the same societal traps repeatedly, you will now discover how to maneuver your way around those pitfalls by using your most powerful weapon; your brain. Your brain is the main control of your body. Your muscles do not think for themselves. They only do what they are told by the brain. Therefore, your brain ultimately directs the body to move according to its instructions before you physically act on anything. The brain has more control over your actions than your peers or environment. Our personalities, hopes, fears and aspirations all depend on the reliability of our brain. There is no way possible to separate the mental from the physical. Essentially, we change whenever the brain changes.

Besides making better decisions as a result of bossing up, you must also learn to move differently than those around you. Do not accept the norms! You must gain confidence in going the opposite way. Stay away from following trends that either put you in a losing position in the long run or trends that go against what you believe in. While existing in a dark place, such as the "hood", you must move cautiously and learn from your mistakes as well as other people's mistakes. Norms in the "hood" include, selling drugs, dropping out of school, consuming numerous drugs, committing white-collar crimes (fraud), having kids at an early age, and fighting. Norms in an unhealthy relationship are unfaithfulness, dishonesty and violence. Norms in a negative learning environment such as school are distractions, disobedience and plagiarism. There is a great chance that your friends and other people around you are heavily involved in more than one of these norms. Before making the mistake of accepting one of these norms, examine those around you who have accepted these norms and analyze their progress. These submissive people are either broke, in jail, dead, lonely or uneducated; you are no exception. Instead of being normal, I suggest that you become great and only make the type of moves that take you forward in life. If you are choosing to boss up, then it is mandatory that you develop a sense of individuality and move differently than others. Always think longevity! The quality of your moves will benefit your prolonged existence. Do what needs to be done now while simultaneously planning for the future.

Growing up, I closely hung out with three guys who were all brothers of each other. One was a fighter, another was a hot-head and the other was younger than all of us, so he was our send off. We easily talked the youngest brother into doing anything. Luckily, we cared about him, so we never persuaded him to do anything too dangerous. I was the cool, somewhat level-headed friend out of the group. As kids, we spent several nights at each other's apartments. I wore their clothes and they wore mine. We partied together; played basketball together, rode around the 'hood together. We did so much together; therefore, we all played contributing roles in each other's foolishness. We were no angels. However, I was always the one that recommended we stop our activities whenever I sensed things were getting too out of hand. They trusted my instincts as much as I trusted them with my life.

The Art of Staying Out the Way

Between the ages of 16-17, there was an incident that forced me to move differently than my friends. One day they found a large amount of cocaine in their mother's deep freezer, which belonged to a man that their mother was dating at the time. They decided that it was financially savvy to shave small portions of cocaine off the top of the large amount that was discovered, so they could sell it. They thought that their mother's boyfriend will never be able to notice that they'd taken it. None of us liked this guy that their mother was dating, so to them it was the right thing to do. I sensed otherwise, but they did not agree with my senses this time. From their perspective, they were just going to sell enough to buy some new gym shoes and clothes for a party that upcoming weekend. I told them that they were "tweakin'" and I was good. In other words, I told them they were making a bad decision and I did not want to have anything to do with it. Sooner or later they started selling drugs on a daily basis out of their mother's backyard to local drug addicts. Eventually, I stopped coming over their home unannounced. Going forward I told them to just call me whenever they were done selling the drugs that they continued to steal, so that we could hang out afterwards.

I still loved my friends, so I did not choose to judge them or write them off completely. Instead, I chose to move differently on my behalf. What they were doing was going against what I believed in and it also was going to put me in a losing position in the long run if I had involved myself. Even though, I totally disagreed with what they were doing, I still drove them around to stores so that they could buy new shoes and clothes every time they made enough money to do so. Perhaps, I contributed to their foolishness by rewarding them with rides to stores whenever they sold enough drugs and made enough money to go shopping. I knew my friends were overall good boys who were now making bad decisions. They were not terrible people. Plus, they were still fun to hang out with whenever they were not selling drugs. Their mother was like my mother and my mother was the same way with them. We were like brothers. Realistically, my friends' bad decisions were not going to cause me to simply end our close relationship with them at that point.

It is sad to say, the entire time I knew what my friends were doing was addictive and had serious consequences because I had first-hand observations of my stepdad living that same destructive lifestyle on a different level. Yet, I could not convince them to see it my way. They simply viewed it as them stealing from a guy that we did not like and making some quick money while doing it. They were hitting a "quick lick". In the end, they got caught. Their mother's boyfriend started noticing the gradual decreases in his drugs. He brought his discovery to their mom's attention and accused her sons of stealing. Their mother approached them with this allegation that her boyfriend had against them. Consequently, my friends' relationship with their mother's boyfriend became further damaged and confrontational.

We all know that fast money is addictive! Even though my friends no longer had any more drugs to steal, they now had an addiction. This addiction was their ultimate downfall. They were now addicted to fast money. Later, one of my friends got arrested for selling drugs and had to do some time at boot camp and the other two were in-and-out the drug game for a period of time. As my friends made more time for selling drugs, there was less time for us to hang out because I continued to move differently. As alternatives, I made more time for school, basketball, part-time and summer jobs, girls and babysitting my little sister. We only hung out whenever it was time to either ride around the 'hood, kick it with some girls, party or shop. Time progressed and we were all between the ages 16-18 years old. Their addiction for fast money and for the lifestyle that came along with it caused our daily routines to slowly grow separate from one another. They were brothers, so they saw each other every day regardless. In my case, the number of days I spent apart from them slowly grew from it just being a couple days to entire week without us hanging out. I still keep contact with three guys today and, fortunately, they have overcome their addiction for fast money finally.

While bossing up, you must understand that you will have to move differently than others around you not because you're better than them, but because you've challenged yourself to think differently. At a given moment, you might have to either move differently than your friends, peers or coworkers as you move forward in life. If you can't convince a friend, family relative or co-worker that there's another level to life, then you must still have confidence in going the other way on your own. You shouldn't judge them nor aggressively persuade them to view life as you now see it. Just do you. In order to make the moves necessary to reach a greater level in our life, then we must first be capable of imagining that there's actually another level to reach. In other words, we must be aware that there are levels in life. However, we all think at a different pace. Hopefully, your friend, family relative or co-worker will soon challenge themselves mentally and move differently too.

Fast forward, there was another situation in which I had to move differently than those around me. This situation occurred later during my junior year in college. Once again, I went to a college that was just 60 miles away from the city. If you went to school, lived or simply partied here and you were from the Westside, then we all cliqued up at some point. On the other hand, there were also cliques created by people who were from the Southside and Eastside. These Eastside and Southside fraternities introduced this college town to white-collar crimes.

They were heavily involved in "cracking cards" (a bank fraud phenomenon) and cell phone fraud schemes. Initially, the Westside fraternity viewed these guys as clowns because of the type of criminal activity they were involved in. In the beginning, these types of crimes were not considered praiseworthy.

However, one day after class I met up with some of the guys from the Westside fraternity as I would normally do. During this time our fraternity house was on a street called Edgebrook. I remember this occasion as clear as day. As I walked into the house, everybody was sitting around in the kitchen. I greeted everyone and shook a couple people's hands; everything was normal up until this point. The next statement that came out of my friend's mouth made our encounter more unusual than any other times. With a smirk on his face, he said "Aye, we about to start doing the cell phone lick." I responded with a smirk on my face as well saying "Bro, you foreal?" He said "yeah, we need some money. But we not gone take it too far like the dudes from the Southside and Eastside. We just gone do a couple phones and that's it." Then, I responded back "bro y'all tweaking. The Feds are all over them dudes from the Southside and Eastside for the same stuff that y'all about to do." As the conversation progressed, I noticed that they were really serious, so I just made it clear that I didn't want to get involved and just told them to be safe.

Similar to my childhood friends, these were also close friends of mine. We shared many similarities and shared many of the same dreams. They were and still are good guys. But fast money is addictive and I understood that! Long story short, they did more than just a couple cell phone scams and, eventually, they graduated to "crackin' cards". As they scheduled more time for participating with fraud schemes, I made more time for school, work and my girlfriend. Using my brain, I comprehended that I had to move differently than them because anything that involved jail as a consequence wasn't a fit for me. I was not a better person than them at the time, but I realized that I had to do what was best for me and that was *staying out the* way. Today, some of those friends are now convicted felons for fraudulent crimes or are felons for doing something illegal that comes along with living that fast lifestyle. I still have much love for them and I wish them the best. Somehow, I hope that we all could come together as winners with legitimate money in the future.

My position isn't to speak down on my friends who made costly mistakes in their lives, but to further illustrate how friends mentally outgrow each other no matter how many concrete similarities they share with one another. This is not about right versus wrong. While bossing up, you must be clear on what's for you and what's not for you. You must be confident in what you believe in and stand for. Sometimes what you believe in may conflict with the norms of your environment or within your peer group. You must be confident in going the other way. Moving differently requires you to make great decisions despite the negative social forces that surround you, so that you will not mistakenly place yourself in a losing situation. Use your brain! Also, you must move differently than how you moved in the past in order to get better results in your future. Your moves must be consistent with your improved way of thinking. Last, I suggest you only make the type of moves that advance your connection with God, family and legitimate money.

The Art of Staying Out the Way

$$\left[\begin{array}{c} \text{Good} \\ \text{Vibes} \\ \text{Only} \end{array} \right]$$

Maneuver #3

After a person chooses to think and move differently, his/her haters will soon begin to reveal themselves. As you move forward in life, you do not leave people behind intentionally. It unintentionally happens for a number of reasons. This is just an ugly truth. These people may eventually become your haters. There is also a thin line between people being inspired by your moves and people being envious of your moves. These jealous-hearted people will become your haters as well. Then, there are going to be people who expected less of you. They wanted you to do good, but not better than them. As you move above their expectations, they began to compare your progression against theirs and will become envious of your success. These spiteful people will also be your haters. Your moves may trigger other people's insecurities. In their minds, you are the ideal picture of how they should have been thinking and moving. They hate to see your growth because it makes them hate themselves even more. These disappointed, insecure people will be your haters too. Bossing up is a challenging task for every person, but it is even harder for stagnant people to do. They will despise the moves you make because they are either too lazy or too uninspired to do what you do. These motionless people will become your haters too. These haters could be friends, strangers and, sad to say, family members as well. While bossing up, it's extremely important that you avoid the haters. Good vibes only!

Bad vibes definitely come from haters, but they have other sources. Doubters provide bad vibes as well. There are going to be people who will doubt your moves and your progression. They will judge your new way of thinking as temporary. Therefore, your moves will be viewed as temporary too. These people do not believe that you could change and, ultimately, succeed beyond the expectations they had set for you. In other words, they cannot foresee you becoming more than what you are. Directly, they will say that you do not know enough, or that you are not good enough. Indirectly, they may ridicule you behind your back to other people, or they just may decide to not acknowledge your growth at all. As a result, their doubt for you will be demonstrated by the lack of support that you receive from them. My mom says doubters are "secret haters". They secretly want you to remain idle in the same position in life. They secretly do not want to see you win. While bossing up, never mind the doubters. Stay close to those who believe in you and who truthfully want to see you do better in life. Good vibes only!

Another source that provides bad vibes is your bad company. Bad company is any person(s) that you are associated with who does not help you move forward in life. These people are the ones that help guide you in harmful, losing situations. They provide negative energy and their negative energy rubs off on you. Keeping bad company around will always hold you back in life. Bad company reinforces bad habits and/or negative lifestyles that you are personally trying to do away with. In other words, bad company motivates you to remain stuck in your old ways by giving you praise for doing something negative. While bossing up, you have to be aware of your bad company. It might be a cousin, friend, co-worker, or stranger who could be bad company for you. If a person either does not want to see you grow, want to help you grow, or want to grow with you, then he/she is dead weight. Fundamentally speaking, if you cannot build with them, then do not chill with them. Good vibes only!

Also, your environment is another source that could provide bad vibes. Specifically, I'm talking about a place /or location that has an unhelpful, negative type of atmosphere. This could be your workplace, your neighborhood, your home, your school, a friend or family relative's house and many other places. Whenever you are at this place, it seems to give off bad energy. You must learn to remove yourself from these places as often as possible. Of course, if it's your home or neighborhood, then it is unrealistic for you to remove yourself instantly and permanently from these places. However, spend as less time as possible there. When you are spending time in a negative environment, just be aware of its negative energy and do not consume it. Stay true to your goals, and remain true to who you are and what you believe in. While bossing up, it's crucial for you to be aware of environments that provide bad vibes and you must remove yourself from these places. Good vibes only!

I have experienced haters, doubters, bad company and negative environments in my life. An example of that was in 2011, I got a job at an athletic footwear store at the Outlet Mall. At this time, I was a 22-year-old junior in college. This was big! I was working at the only mall that was near my college campus for one of its popular stores. The Outlet Mall had so many popular stores. This outlet mall was close to 30 miles away from my college campus. Still, everyone made this almost 30-mile drive from the college campus to the Outlet Mall whenever it was time to shop for an outfit to wear to a party or after refund checks got disbursed to students. The stores in the small college town were only good for grocery shopping and buying house appliances. There were not any stores in town where students could shop for fly shoes or clothing. For that reason, the fashionable thing to do was to go to the Outlet Mall.

You could imagine how this outlet mall was the hotspot and I was working there! Beautiful females flooded this outlet mall and guys naturally followed. Since I was working at a store that sold popular gym shoes, I made contact with the majority of these beautiful women. Plus, I had an employee discount that I could use as leverage. If there was a female that I had a form of friendship with, or if there was a female that I thought was beautiful, I allowed them to use my employee discount with their purchase. I did not do this every time to get their phone numbers as an exchange for my discount. I mostly did it because they were either my friends or because I just enjoyed helping beautiful women in general. This job put me in my glory! I was "the man" on a certain level that did not involve me risking my freedom or life. At the beginning, I was truly grateful for my job and I worked extremely hard on every shift. I was a sales floor associate, which meant I provided customer service and maintained a clean store. Every shift, I was authentically helping customers, folding t-shirts, organizing shoes and/or putting clothes back on hangers. I never had an issue with working hard. I worked hard not only because I enjoyed working around beautiful women, but because that is naturally who I am and that's a hard worker.

    Fast forward, a few months go by and I began to sense bad vibes amongst my coworkers and leadership. Yet, I was still enjoying the female customers as well as my employee discount. I started to encounter haters, doubters and bad company amongst my coworkers and leadership. It became a negative work environment. (Josh if you ever decide to read this book I specifically want you to know that this bad vibe didn't involve you bro! Josh was one of my coworkers at the shoe store who inspired me and shared some of the same interests that I had. He is one of the coolest Puerto Ricans I've ever met thus far.) Majority of my other coworkers and leadership were residents near the Outlet Mall. These were mainly adults and a small portion was high school or college students whose schools were located close to the Outlet Mall. It was not a secret amongst my coworkers that I was a junior in college. I never announced my academic situation in a bragging manner. School simply came up in passing conversations while we were working. I have never bragged about me going to school at any point in my life because I was instructed by my mother that pursuing an education is expected of people for their own wellbeing. Instead, how a person applies his/her education is more praiseworthy.

While at work, there were times when I would complain at times to my coworkers and leadership about the long drive from my college campus to work and about the amount of homework or studying that I had to complete after work. My junior year in college was a reality check. It was time to set goals, pick a major and take my future more seriously. Therefore, I use to vent about it from time to time. That is mainly how my coworkers and leadership were made aware of my college situation. There were many instances in which my adult coworkers and leadership tried to throw shade over my situation. For the sake of continuing the progress of this chapter, I've decided to only share a couple instances. One day, I was assigned to work a 5 a.m. shift, which was the shift when pricing and stocking were both done. In order to move quicker on this shift, we had a slight assembly line set up. One person priced an item while the next another person applied a theft detector and the last person put the item on a hanger. While we priced and stocked items, we conversed with one another. Long story short, we got on the topic of college. My 28-35 year old coworkers, who were folding clothes and putting price stickers on items, collectively said that college was a waste of time in so many words. They were avid about their disdain for pursuing a college education in hope that it discourages me.

Also, I got bad vibes from one of the assistant managers. In the beginning, she was actually cool. She was very easy on the eyes. Anyways, after a few months of me being employed there, she went back to school to obtain a degree in business. She and I talked briefly about college every now-and-then because that became our common ground. Whenever we conversed with one another, she always made it her business to draw comparison between her academic situation and mine. The assistant manager was outwardly insecure of her age; she was in her late-20s around the time she decided to go to college. Occasionally, she compared her academic situation against the younger employees. Her debate was that she made the best decision compared to younger people who were in college because, unlike us, she was already in her career as an Assistant Manager and a business degree will only further her position in the retail business. Whenever we would get on this topic, I responded by clearly expressing how and why I was still confident with my journey despite her argument. My confidence startled her.

One day as we were sitting in her office, we were counting my drawer because I was assigned to be the cashier that day, she made an attempt to further enlighten me. She pulled up a list of applicants who were applying for a position at this specific shoe store on her computer. These applicants all had college degrees. My response was "Ok, so what does this suppose to mean?" She responded by saying "so many young people with college degrees apply for this job" with the purpose of strengthening her academic situation. This incident bothered me. After this encounter, she and I had many more heated debates about this topic. My position was that everyone's journey is different and the only thing that matters is that they eventually reach their goals. I made it clear to her that, regardless of what she thought, I was going to still become successful. Her idea of success was different from mine. However, it was clear to me that her objective was to discourage me while simultaneously uplifting her. It was mind-blowing! Not only was I receiving a bad vibe from a few coworkers, but from my leadership as well. I was working amongst haters, doubters and bad company.

While experiencing these bad vibes, I use to call my mother often so that I could vent to her about them. I expressed how my job had become a negative work environment due to the bad vibes that my coworkers and leadership had created with their negative energy. Honestly, it reached a point where I started to feel drained after working every shift at this job. I used to tell my momma that I had to remove myself from this environment as soon as possible. She would try to encourage me to keep my job, but learn to ignore the haters and doubters. And that is exactly what I chose to do. However, the hate and doubt that was coming from my coworkers and leadership seemed to grow even louder. I expressed to my mother that I was not sure about how much longer I could work in such an environment. At this point, my mother now encouraged me to have another job in place before quitting my current job. She could sense the job was really draining my good energy.

Later, I decided to walk away from the job. It was no place for a young-optimistic person like me. I had to remove myself from this negative environment and from around those kinds of people in order to protect my good energy. Unfortunately, I did not have another job in place when I decided to walk away from the job. Instead, I had a college graduation and internship that required my utmost attention. Around the time I decided to quit my job, my college graduation and internship were both three months away. In my mind, both were more valuable than pursuing another part-time job during that time. So I decided to preserve my good energy for those tasks that brightened my future. Fortunately, I had enough money saved to support myself those following months while I was unemployed.

I am not suggesting that anyone quit their job nor am I recommending anyone to not work a part-time job while in college. I made this personal choice to quit my job because of the negative work environment and I could also afford to do so. I was a 23-year old and a slightly impulsive person, but I was undeniably fed up. I could not bear it anymore. Still, I had a plan. My plan was to step away from that job, so that I could focus more on graduating from college and prepare for my internship without any distractions. Also, my plan was to wisely budget the money that I had saved throughout my employment period. My plan was not the best or very thorough, but at least I had one. Therefore, I am instead suggesting that you put together a concrete plan before making a permanent decision such as quitting your job. If the bad vibe in your environment has become intolerable (infinite haters, doubters, bad company, etc), then this should be all the motivation you need that should push you to relentlessly maneuver your way out of that situation.

Admittedly, I must give credit to the dark place that I described earlier. This place taught me much of what I had to know about maneuvering around bad vibes. So the decision I had to make at that job was tough, but was nothing new. While growing up in the "hood", I was surrounded by so many destructive mindsets like the ones I described in the earlier chapter (bad company). Some teachers, adults and peers doubted that I will ever make it out the 'hood alive or as a free man (doubters). And if they did not doubt me, then others had low expectations for me such as them only encouraging me to graduate from of high school. Also, hate is plays a major role in the 'hood. People will not only hate you what you've accomplished, but will also hate you for having a new pair of gym shoes and/or a new outfit. They will even hate your talents and accomplishments. In the 'hood, people find any reason to hate (haters). Therefore, I've been maneuvering through life surrounded by haters, doubters, bad company and negative environments since a child. I'm capable of using all of my senses for recognizing bad vibes and skillfully maneuvering away from the negativity.

Good vibes only! In short, a vibe is a person's emotional state or the atmosphere of a place as communicated to and felt by others. Positive people generate positive energy that, in turn, helps create an encouraging atmosphere that is needed for a person to fully flourish and move forward in life. I had to realize that there's limited space in my lifetime and this space should only be filled with people that's either going to make me laugh, make me happy, keep me focused and/or keep me motivated. Also, regardless of my environment, I must preserve my positive energy and don't allow other people's negative energy to influence me. If I'm living or working in a negative environment or amongst negative people, then this should further motivate me to grind much harder to move forward in life so that I won't have to deal with this same environment or these same people for much longer. Bad vibes keep us down while good vibes lift us up. The choice is yours.

The Art of Staying Out the Way

Maneuver #4

While bossing up, do not be afraid of moving alone for God is always with us. The circumstances around you may make you feel like you are alone and weak. The people around you may not fully recognize your vision, so you may feel disconnected. If you have friends, business partners and/or family members who are not as interested in bossing up as you are, then do not become discouraged when you find yourself doing it alone. Initially, you might have to begin your journey alone until you are fortunate enough to find some people that bring you good vibes. God said "I will never leave thee, nor forsake you" (Hebr. 13:5 King James Version). You must allow God's unseen presence to comfort you throughout your journey. Have faith in God. Have faith while maneuvering solo!

Ideally, we are an interdependent society. Our interdependence is what makes the world go round. We all depend on each other for particular services. However, you may periodically have to single-handedly get things done on your own! Whenever you finally decide to boss up, you might not have enough support surrounding you to begin with. You have envisioned more for yourself, but others cannot fathom you being more than what you already are. You have envisioned more for your peers, coworkers and/or family as well, but they refuse to grasp the fact that there is more out there for them. As a result, you are forced to maneuver on your own. It takes nothing to stand in a crowd; it takes everything to stand alone. Truthfully, it's not always fun being alone. But it is even more punishing when you to try to thrive around people who either do not recognize your greatness, people who do not inspire you and/or around people who are not willing to grind with you. At this point, you will have to grind alone and, eventually, you will cross paths with supportive people as you move forward through your journey.

My senior year in high school, there was a situation in which I had to maneuver solo. Throughout high school, I hung out with a specific group of friends. Their names were Lil Ant, J.R., Square and Sterlo. These were my best friends and we did everything together. We went to class together, partied together, fought together and everything else.

You name it, we did it! I even had a relationship with their mothers and they had one with mine. Whenever one of us wasn't answering the phone for our mother, then our mothers will call any one of our cell phones in order to find out where their son was and why he wasn't answering his phone. During my sophomore year, there was an incident when I didn't answer several of my mother's phone calls. I was at this beautiful girl's house, she was a junior at the time, and we were having a crazy kissing session. My mom called my friends' phones looking for me. All of them told my mother that they were not aware of my whereabouts. Truthfully, they all knew that I was at this girl's house, but they just didn't want my mother to know because this was a huge win for the team. Whenever one of us hung out with a girl that we all thought was fine, then it was like a team win for us. However, my mom's intuition told her that my friends were lying. Later, she expressed how disappointed she was with them and I also was put on a short punishment.

In short, that explains our friendship. We were close, and we were willing to win and lose together. That changed toward the end of our senior year in high school. A few months prior to graduation, school counselors became more visible and reachable. Also, a few navy and army recruiters begin became present in the school. We were finally being challenged to choose who we wanted to become and what we wanted to do in the future. It was time for us to choose our paths in life. I sat in my school counselor's office and spoke with him for the first time. He was known for wearing cowboy boots. He asked me about college. Instantly, I had a flashback of a conversation that I had with my older cousin D-Live while I was in the eighth grade. Around this time, my cousin D-Live was a student at a university. He told me, "Junior, go to college! In my dormitory, I got a girl on every floor!" So when my school counselor asked me about college, I simply replied that I was interested. I gave him a couple of university names that I knew of. First, I mentioned a university that my cousin MeMe was attending. I also told him that I knew about another university located Down South because I overheard my friend J.R. talking about this university in the past. Other than that, I really did not know anything about college. With the help of my school counselor, I applied to both colleges. I was later accepted into the college where my cousin MeMe was attending through its Risk Program, a program that gives public school students with low grade point averages a chance to attend their university.

As planned, after graduating from high school, I went to a college that was 60 miles away from home to further my education because I heard that was where the most beautiful girls were in the state of Illinois. I made this move alone! My friend J.R. went to college Down South, Sterlo and Lil Ant joined the Navy, and Square stayed home. We all did our own thing in hope that we all could bring a trophy back home and celebrate a team victory in the end. I was far from fearful about going away to college alone. As long as there were girls there, I was going to be fine. Plus, I had a plan. My plan was to simply do well in every class and find some new-good vibes. Truth be told, I did not go off to college with a studious plan. I did not go with the ideal "American Dream" in mind. At the time, I was not convinced that graduating from college made a person either better or richer than the next man. Essentially, I went to college because of the girls, I knew that I could handle the workload and because I wanted to continue to make my mother proud.

While attending college, there were still occasions when I had to maneuver solo. My freshman year, I was fortunate enough to find some good vibes. I found a group of friends that shared the same interests as I had and they were all from the Westside like me. We walked around the college campus as deep as a basketball team at times! There were numerous occasions when almost fifteen of us would collectively go to the Recreation Center with a group of girls following behind us. Plenty of us knew how to play basketball, so we would enter the gym with our takeover attitude. T had a crazy crossover, S Dot had an automatic jump shot, Capo had old And1 moves, Tuck was the most energetic and physical person on the court, Speedy was all-around nice, and I had a decent jump shot and could drive to the rim with ease. That's just to name a few of us. Plus, we were all cool, fly and good looking according to the ladies. So we kept some fine cheerleaders on the sideline rooting for us. We turned the gym up every time we were there!

Freshman year, we attended parties, visited different dormitories, kicked it with girls, went to class, played basketball and, sometimes, did homework collectively as a group. One of us never explored the campus alone because typically we had drama with other sets of friends throughout campus. The root of our drama with other sets of friends was either due to one of us was talking to one of their girlfriends or due to outright senselessness. Therefore, we moved as a team. I was surrounded by so many good vibes that I soon forgot about my friends back home as a result. I rarely traveled back home during my freshman year in college. Every day I went to class, kicked it with my boys and, then, spent the night with a girl.

Gradually, these good vibes faded away. Sophomore year, controversy regarding disloyalty and other disagreements amongst my friends caused our group to become divided. Some of my friends also dropped out of college. One by one they returned home while I furthered my education. Those walks to class in a huge group of guys that once provided good vibes became walks alone to class. I had to maneuver solo not because I was smarter than my friends, but because I was the only one who decided not to drop out. Again, I did not believe that I was going to become better or richer than my friends because I simply chose to stay in college and they did not. At the time, I was still convinced that college did not make a person better or richer than the next man. Personally, I simply viewed me getting a college degree as the next thing to do in life after high school. Despite my friends dropping out, I was still able to boss up alone.

It was tough going from a lot of friends to having to be solo because my resiliency was challenged. My ability to go to class, to the gym and travel across campus alone after once doing all of this with my friends was a true test. Also, I was more so bothered by my friends not having a plan outside of getting a college education. A few of them were much smarter than I was, so they weren't quitting because they weren't intelligent enough to finish. Still, I put my head down and push forward! When it was time to party, I could always count on those friends to be available. When it was time to take care of business around campus, I did so relentlessly. I had to be extremely disciplined and positive in order to graduate from college. I encouraged myself to keep going every day, patted myself on the back after I passed a test or completed an assignment and found true happiness within myself.

I stayed true to what I believed in, which was to continue to move forward in life. Ten years from now, I do not want to reflect back on life and have a bunch of "what if's". Therefore, I wanted to check "get a college degree" off my to-do list just in case it benefited me later in life. And that's exactly what I did. At graduation, I was the only person out of my original group of friends from freshman year to graduate from college. I say this to say, that there are times in life that will require us to single-handedly get things done. Have faith while maneuvering solo!

I will like to add that we should not be alone in life. Alone could become scary and could be depressing. We must find good people to move forward with in life. Much more could be done by a group of people rather than one person alone. Life is harder whenever we try to do everything on our own. If you have a dream, then your dream could easily become a reality with the help from others. While maneuvering solo, we must simultaneously search for good vibes and, also, embrace the good vibes that we already have.

The Art of Staying Out the Way

"The Westside Fraternity"

The Art of Staying Out the Way

$$\left[\begin{array}{c} \text{Remind} \\ \\ \text{Yourself} \end{array} \right]$$

MANEUVER #5

As a young black male who has come from a dark place and who is constantly provoked by the darkness, both physically and mentally, I frequently have to remind myself of those previous maneuvers. I try to be as self-reflective as possible, so that I can continuously identify my mistakes or identify my barriers. Then, learn from my mistakes or learn to maneuver around any barriers. I become a better person or put myself in a better position as a result. The *Art of Staying Out the Way* requires us to constantly identify, learn and then grow. We must identify our mistakes and/or our barriers, learn from our slip-ups or learn how to maneuver around societal barriers and then, use what we have learned to move forward in life. We must be mentally present throughout our journey. While bossing up, it's crucial that we practice consistency. Consistently, we must remind ourselves that we're bossing up and, therefore, we must think and move accordingly.

Not too long ago, I tuned into an interview that went viral. It was a radio interview that was aired across the internet. The radio station is a nationally syndicated hit radio show because the show has a massive following and many celebrities are featured on its morning show. Throughout this specific interview, the interviewee constantly refocused the discussion whenever he felt as if he was being misunderstood by saying

"Pause". I thought it was very effective! He relentlessly tried his best to explain to the interviewers what being a boss consisted of. The discussion went sour on a few occasions. Every time there seemed to be a disagreement or misunderstanding, the interviewee quickly froze the discussion by saying "pause" before he further attempted to passionately provide clarity. This interview was very powerful. It is evident that the interviewee has spent his entire life "bossing up" with respect to his obvious accomplishments over the years, such as his success with his legendary record company. Specifically, the manner in which the interviewee used the term "pause" could be put into practice while executing the maneuver for Reminding Yourself.

There will be times when you have to pause, and then remind yourself what it means to be a boss. A boss is in charge of his/her destiny. A boss manages his/her own belief system. A boss has far-out expectations and goals set for him/her. Remind yourself that a boss is expected to be aware of all the positives and negatives that surround him/her. A boss's demeanor is shaped by a high level of self-worth. Along with a boss's confidence is great awareness. A boss does a great job of examining every situation thoroughly, so that he/she will not mistakenly place himself in a losing position. A boss has a mind of his/her own. God, family, progress and money all occupy a boss's mental framework, which leaves no space for drama. A boss places value on his mental wealth as well as his financial wealth. Constant thinking is what allows a boss to constantly move up levels in life. Every potential move is thought about realistically, so this means a boss considers both favored outcomes as well unpleasing outcomes before making a decision.

There have been plenty of times in which I had to pause and think about what I was doing or about to do. Also, there have been numerous of instances in which I had to pause and pay closer attention to what was happening around me. I had to mentally tell myself to "pause", so that I could clearly identify, learn and grow.

Growing up in a dark place, the uncertainties were plentiful because there were societal barriers and pitfalls everywhere! For instance, when I was 12 years old I lived with my mother, stepfather and sister on Augusta and Lamon St. on Chicago's Westside. I quickly met a couple kids who were around the same age as me and they were both boys too, but I don't recall their names. They stayed approximately two or three buildings to the right of my apartment building. In the beginning, we joked and played around every time we met up. We practiced our basketball handles, practiced wrestling moves, threw rocks and, whenever it was too hot outside, we would play each other's video games. It was good vibes whenever we were around one another. As time went along, we learned more about each other. Soon, I learned that these two boys' families were traditionally gang affiliated. I don't remember the exact gang, but both kids' families shared the same gang affiliation. They spoke passionately about this! At the time, I was only aware of drugs. My family's connection with drugs involved both dealing and using. We had a couple family members who actively sold drugs and we had a couple other family members who actively used drugs. On the other hand, I wasn't really aware of gangs just yet. When I saw guys standing on corners, I viewed them as drug dealers rather than gang members. Therefore, I was slightly clueless during the times these two boys spoke on the topic of gangs.

Eventually, they asked me if I wanted to join their family's gang. It was almost as if they had asked me to join their family. I was into gym shoes, video games, basketball and girls as a child my age should. Joining a gang never crossed my mind until these boys mentioned it. Without much thought, I replied "yeah" when they asked me if I wanted to join their gang. They responded, "OK, tomorrow we gotta bless you in." The following day I met up with them. They said "Ok, we gone bless you in our hallway." I responded "Ok, come on." Their hallway had two flights of stairs. I stood in between these two flights. These two boys pulled out a yellow, plastic baseball bat. They asked "you ready?" I responded "ready for what?" Then, they said "we gotta hit you 30 times with this bat because that's how we bless new members into the gang. Our uncles taught us this." Without thinking at all, I said "Ok, come on. But don't hit me too hard." So they started swinging "1, 2, 3, 4..." The hits became harder and harder. I yelled "HOLD ON" because the hits were starting to sting.

At that moment, I mentally told myself to pause as well told them to physically pause. The situation became clearer to me as I started to wrap my brain around it. Clearly, this was a bad situation! I told them that I'd changed my mind and demanded that they stop. They responded "if you don't get all 30 of these hits, then you can't be in our gang." I replied "I don't care, y'all tripping." As I was replying, I was also making my way down the flight of stairs and out the door. They followed behind me with the yellow, plastic bat in a joking manner. But I was dead serious! Once I made it home and sat down, I started to reflect on what happened previously. While reflecting, I identified that I almost made a terrible mistake by volunteering to join a gang that I knew nothing about and clearly this gang involved violence. I wasn't a violent person, so their gang didn't compliment what I believed in at the time. At that time, I exclusively believed in playing video games, playing basketball, wearing nice gym shoes with matching clothes and talking to girls. Also, while reflecting, I learned how my own mistakes could put me in harm's way. Those two didn't force me into their hallway, I volunteered to be there. Therefore, I voluntarily put myself in harm's way. After reflecting, I vowed to never put myself in another losing situation ever again. I was able to grow as a better person because of this life altering experience. As a result, I heightened my level of self-awareness. In the future, if something is neither beneficial nor cool to me, then I promised myself that I will never voluntarily involve myself with that something.

Fast forward and years later I still have to remind myself to *stay out the way* as a 23-year old college graduate. When I returned home from college, I was excited! I was a college graduate and I was back home ready to hit the streets! There were 24-inch rims on my car, so I was ready to "get in traffic". I quickly encountered a phenomenon that was specifically popular on the Westside of Chicago. This was the "FeFe" phenomenon. I am aware that there are many different meanings for the term "FeFe", but the Westside coined their own meaning for the term. The word "FeFe" is an abbreviation for fiesta. A fiesta is an event marked by festivities or celebration that takes place outside. People gather up outside and party together. There is liquor, illegal substances, music and dancing involved. A "FeFe" typically takes place near a park, on a corner or along an entire street. The disadvantage of a "FeFe" is the potential number of guns that are most likely present and the violent chaos that frequently occurs at this event.

That summer when I returned home, I was going to "FeFe's" like crazy! I was only going to show off my clean car, clean outfit, clean shoes, and clean haircut. I also went to kick it with my guys and to be around females. After a couple months of going to "FeFe's", I realized that I was ultimately putting myself in dangerous situations. I came to this realization after having a "pause moment". I was at a "FeFe" on Jackson and Springfield. This night I was extremely bored, so I instinctively listened to other people's conversations that were taking place around me. To the right of where I was standing, one guy was explaining to his friend how he would shoot anybody that was out there. Behind me, a female was telling her friend that she will only date "savages" with dreadlocks. And to my far left, I overheard another guy bragging about how many different drugs he had consumed that night. Overall, there were always guns, gangs, drugs and some ignorant people throughout these "FeFe's", but I did not consider my safety initially because I was too busy drinking, talking and laughing instead. After hearing those conversations and paying closer attention to my surroundings, I quickly realized that I was at the wrong party. I was once again putting myself in harm's way voluntarily. If any harm was done to me while at a "FeFe", then I would have been partially liable for my damages because I voluntarily chose to expose myself to that evil by simply choosing to be there. My family could not have rationally placed full blame on anyone or any circumstance because of my involvement.

After gradually going forward in life for so long, I was mentally in a different space. I had no room for negativity or negative thoughts. My mental space was filled with happiness, peace, encouragement and positivity and I am going to take the necessary step in order to keep it that way. My experiences gained in college contributed to a large portion of my mental growth. It exposed me to different people and different ways of living. Also, graduating from college was confirmation that I had the ability to get things done in life. As a result, college boosted my confidence and I also became accustomed to having fun and being around beautiful people. I was not interested in shooting anyone or using a variety of drugs when I came back home. Physically, I still wore popular gym shoes and had rims on my car, but I had different state of mind compared to my mindset that I had prior my college experience. The other 50% of my mental growth was the result of me personally challenging myself throughout life. Since I was younger I have challenged myself to always stay true to what I believe in. I have always believed in going forward in life, looking good, being happy and living a harmless lifestyle. I never believed in selling drugs, shooting, and/or stealing.

On the other hand, people who attended these "FeFe's" readily embraced negative energy. Mentally, it just seemed as if our states of mind were completely different. It took me a while to become levelheaded, but it appeared as if some people at these "FeFe's" were neither interested in bossing up nor aware of their mediocre, destructive lifestyle. Once again, I have never been convinced that college made me a better person than those people who chose not to go. I just believe that certain activities and thinking patterns simply get played out in due time and I learned that during and after college. The things that they were doing and saying at these "FeFe's" were so played out from perspective. For instance, if a person was high, drunk and off a pill at the same time, then his capacity to consumed all those drugs was viewed as an accomplishment at these events. Everybody high-fived him! If you were willing to shoot a person, then you were "a somebody". There were even some people who still wore super baggy clothes. The year was 2013, but it seemed as if some people were still mentally trapped in the year 2007-2008. Let me be clear, I'm not mocking anyone. But when I "paused" and clearly evaluated the situation, I became frustrated with those people at these "FeFe's" who weren't bossing up! Also, I became frustrated with myself for voluntarily putting myself in harm's way.

After pausing and reflecting, I identified that I was simply going to the wrong parties. I don't like to judge people, so I purely acknowledged that I was hanging around the wrong scenes instead of making the judgment that I was around the wrong people. Next, I learned that I had to stop going to these "FeFe's" and found alternative events that were safer. Many people were either shot, robbed or victims of other senseless acts while attending these "FeFe's". I was fortunate enough to avoid those troubles because I chose to stop putting myself in harm's way. I had to remind myself of my worth and that I had a purpose in life.

While at these "FeFe's", I was surrounding myself around vibes that were detrimental to my wellbeing. Fortunately, I was able to remind myself that my life is worth more than what was offered to me at a "FeFe." Even though I do enjoy music, dancing, kicking it with my guys and being around beautiful women, I must continue to remind myself that there are levels! I must enjoy those types of festivities on a safer level. I had came to the conclusion that I couldn't party like I use to when I was 16-17 years old; I had to move forward and party like a boss.

Constantly remind yourself that you do not have to do what everyone is doing. Find your own path. While bossing up, remind yourself that you are only going forward in life. If there's anything, any person, or any place that cause you to go backwards, then it isn't good for you. Remind yourself to think differently. Think differently than how you did in the past, especially if the way you thought in the past hindered you. Only make moves according to your new way of thinking. Don't move like the old you because the old you didn't get you anywhere. Your new objective is to get somewhere in life.

A "FeFe" on the Westside of Chicago; An outside gathering that is meant to be joyous but it's very dangerous a lot of times.

> *Stay out the way & Work!*

MANEUVER #6

The phrase *stay out the way* is a maneuver in itself. Specifically, this technique is for any person who constantly avoids barriers, pitfalls, traps and evils. Barriers, pitfalls, traps and evils could be found throughout various 'hoods, suburbs, jobs, college campuses, homes and relationships. Relatively speaking, to stay out the way is to stay away from any barriers, pitfalls, traps and evils. *Staying out the way* requires a person to be aware, disciplined, proactive and reflective. First, a person must be aware of any barriers, pitfalls, traps and evils that surround him/her. Then, he/she must be disciplined enough to not go near those things. This requires a person to become proactive about avoiding those harmful things. While *staying out the way*, there may be some instances when a person makes a few mistakes by going near or actually involving him/herself with these barriers, pitfalls, traps and evils. He/she must then have the capacity to be reflective, so that person could learn to grow from his/her mistakes and misfortunes.

With regards to those who are concerned about the origins of this phrase, this phrase has been culturally coined in this manner. "Staying out the way" is an urban phrase that's been historically used to caution people that there is harm or consequences that they need to be aware of and essentially avoid. The concept *of staying out the way* is encouraging everyone to remain safe, drama-free, proactive, hopeful, goal-oriented and conscious. To say the least, we must keep away from drugs, guns, hate, doubt, bad company, bad vibes, stagnation, hopelessness, irrational thinking and peer pressure. In the prior chapters I offered maneuvers that will further help a person *stay out the way*. These maneuvers are applicable in many other settings rather than exclusively the 'hood. I shared short stories in which I used these maneuvers while in the 3rd grade, high school, college and while in a job and 'hood setting.

I am a firm believer in *the art of staying out the way*. I breathe it, I live it and I speak it fluently. I have a few hiccups every now and then, but that is because I'm human. Essentially, *staying out the way* is a lifestyle. Whenever I neglect this lifestyle, the consequences are instant. *Staying out the way* is a much harder lifestyle compared to a person who lives carelessly. A careless person typically hit barriers, falls into pitfalls and/or usually become victim to society's traps. On the other hand, a person who practices *the art of staying out the way* typically maneuver through life cautiously. In order to be cautious, this requires a person to be aware, disciplined, proactive and reflective. This lifestyle demands constant work! Therefore, I am also a firm believer in the fact that hard work will get anyone far in life. Keep in mind that our prime objective is to go further while bossing up.

Stay out the way & Work! It is very important for us to both stay busy and stay working as well. *The art of staying out the way* only keeps us in a position to win. After we are in position, we must then put effort into actually winning. If we're too busy working, then it is less likely for us to have any additional time to voluntarily affect ourselves with society's barriers, pitfalls, traps and evils. In order for us to stay busy and stay working, then we must be goal-oriented. There's so much work that could be done in our lifetime. Work a job, work on completing school, do work around the house, work on your jump shot, work on your vocals, work on an invention, work on improving your relationship with family/friends, work on your drawing or writing skills, work on building a website, work on a science project and, most importantly, continue to work on yourself. Work, work, and work some more! I believe that good things come to those who work for them.

Currently, I am staying out the way of more than just fights, gangs, drugs, and things of that nature. Nowadays, there is a greater need for me to stay out the way of self-doubt, mediocrity, stagnation, selfishness, ignorance, racism and envious people. There are times when I am my own bad company. Whenever I doubt myself, I cause myself to become stagnant. Self-doubt and stagnation both keep me trapped in the same position in life, but I remind myself that a boss is expected to move forward.

I am aware that society wants me to settle for mediocrity. I believe that none of us were born to become average. Without a doubt, graduating from college and obtaining a full-time job with benefits were great accomplishments. However, my mother passionately lectured and embedded in my belief system that getting an education and obtaining a job are actions expected of a person. While those are great accomplishments, there are many other goals that I will accomplish in my lifetime. I am continuously and constantly challenging myself to *stay out the way* of mediocrity and strive for greatness.

I could be selfish while striving for greatness. There are days when I only focus on my individual goals without considering what other people have going on around me. Perhaps, those people need my help. I'm learning to *stay out the way* of my selfish habits and become more considerate of others. Last, there is ignorance, racism and envy everywhere. I am trying extremely hard to keep away from those evils.

I am working extremely hard too. Currently, I'm one semester away from graduating with my Master's Degree; I have a full-time career job and I'm in the process of executing ideas. Also, I am now elevating *the practice of bossing up* to another level. Before the year ends, I should have my first piece of real estate. Being a first-time home buyer is exciting, confusing, fulfilling and scary altogether. There's so much for me to learn because I don't have enough background knowledge about mortgage loans, building or renovating a home, credit scores, interest rates and all that other stuff. On the other hand, I definitely do know how to stack my money. I've been working and stacking my money, so that I could eventually invest and become an owner. My goal is to invest money into buying my first two-flat building before the year 2015 ends. Set that goal and go get it! Most importantly, I am currently putting consistent work into improving the person I am both personally and professionally. Personally, I could be a better son, grandson, brother, boyfriend, nephew, cousin and friend. Professionally, my communication skills could be better. I need to get as much work done as I possibly can while I'm young. I had my fun as a young person should, but now I am focused on getting things accomplished. I prefer to work hard now and chill later.

Last Encouraging Thoughts

I encourage everyone to never be intimidated by the darkness. The darkness is just a test and we must pass through it. Even though it might be a struggle, continue to move forward. Going forward is the ultimate answer for any situation. The choice is yours. Love yourself, love what's yours and love your process. Everyone's process is unique from one another.

The Art of Staying Out the Way is an expression that is encouraging everyone to keep away from negativity. Negativity has its way of sucking life out of a person. Negativity comes from various sources. Be aware of those sources and avoid them. On the other hand, positivity is the key to happiness. Positivity also involves us encouraging one another to be great. We were given life to do something great. We have the ability to become all that we wish to be only if we honestly apply ourselves. The world needs us because we all have something that we could offer. Stay positive, enjoy life, give back and be great!

t.a.o.s.o.t.w

PLEDGE ON *STAYING OUT THE WAY*

I pledge to *stay out the way*

Of all barriers, pitfalls, traps and evils

I am aware that I have power as long as I have a choice

No darkness shall prevail

I will exercise my choice to outshine any darkness

Failure is not an option

And the only option is to keep going forward

As long as I keep God first, no darkness will last

Success is inevitable

I will succeed as long as I *stay out the way*

I will forever remain positive through tough times

Staying out the way is a lifestyle

I will stay true to this lifestyle

Even when this lifestyle isn't the most convenient

I will have a meaningful life because I have a purpose

As long as I live my life's purpose, I will succeed

Love.

The Art of Staying Out the Way

(The Worksheet)

Identify (What are my barriers, pitfalls, traps and/evils?):

Learn (How could I avoid them?):

Grow (Why would this improve my position?):

The Art of Staying Out the Way

(The Worksheet)

Identify (What are my flaws?):

Learn (How could I improve them?):

Grow (Why would these improvements develop who I am as a person?)

The Art of Staying Out the Way

(The Worksheet)

Apply each maneuver to a situation of yours.

Maneuver #1 (Boss Up):

Maneuver #2 (Move Differently):

Maneuver #3 (Good Vibes Only):

Maneuver #4 (S O L O):

Maneuver #5 (Remind Yourself):

Maneuver #6 (*Stay out the way* & Work!):

The Art of Staying Out the Way

(The Worksheet)

Apply each maneuver to a situation of yours.

Maneuver #1 (Boss Up):

Maneuver #2 (Move Differently):

Maneuver #3 (Good Vibes Only):

Maneuver #4 (S O L O):

Maneuver #5 (Remind Yourself):

Maneuver #6 (*Stay out the way* & Work!):

Summary of Instructions

Step 1: Boss Up

Step 2: Move Differently

Step 3: Good Vibes Only

Step 4: S O L O

Step 5: Remind Yourself

Step 6: *Stay out the way* and Work!

Repeat these steps as often as needed.

t.a.o.s.o.t.w

a DreSmitti creation

t.a.o.s.o.t.w

a DreSmitti creation

The Art of Staying Out the Way